Not Just Love

A Selection of 100 Poems

Mojibur Rahman

Eloquent Books
New York, New York

Eloquent Books
An imprint of AEG Publishing Group
845 Third Avenue, 6th Floor - 6016
New York, NY 10022
www.eloquentbooks.com

ISBN: 978-1-60860-331-2

Printed in the United States of America

I dedicate this book to all who strive to bring justice and fairness among the oppressed peoples of the world.

Acknowledgements

I am very grateful to Dorothy Winters for her meticulous and painstaking endeavour in going through these poems and her comments. I am also thankful to Rose Williams and Jill Beadon for their suggestions and feedback. I must also acknowledge the positive comments offered by the editorial team of a publisher of classic and contemporary work.

Contents

Poems Are Born!

Poems are born!
Out of mind's womb.
To show our pleasure
doom and gloom.

Poems are born!
Chained in words and phrases.
Slaves of hopes and desires
in the grip of the ages.

An eye of imagination
glance at the face of decay.
And the acts of time
turns the love of life away.

The true conquest
loss of love and pains.
Seeds of sin beset
all values tied to chains.

Mouth of urge is dry
and care drips into blood.
Mind agreeable may deny
the sap of words to flood.

With inhibition and strife
warring words born to fight.
Contrived to live its own life
or ordained to shoot at sight.

Poems may be the cradle of peace
or just to show how much I love you.
It could just be a disguise to say.
Oh yes I do! And oh yes I do.

Poems act or play a part
at the fiery stage of life.
Paints like a brush in art
faces of all human strife.

Quantum Leap

Affairs of a quantum leap
reaching to a height beyond belief.
Is there a limit of its progress?
Where to stop and regress.

To be with the rise
matching moves are in need.
Out of step and wheel clamps
and growth grinds to a halt.

Skill is a factor for
helping or failing the scheme.
Large or small in scale
a choice has to be made.

A leap in the dark
or in the pool of progress.
Makes fate of the people
to receive more or less.

Hardly Know the Man

Susie and Clare are after Lenny
squabbling to claim his heart.
Susie warns Clare not to kiss
making it public like Exchange and Mart.
There is no need for you to fight.
Susie tells Clare to ban
making an excuse for a light.
Clare replies, I hardly know the man.

Susie goes through restless nights.
Bearing the pain of first love.
Love that is not only her life
but all around below and above.
Clare is just using Lenny
to make her boyfriend jealous.
What else could she do
when James plays to be so callous?

Susie badly wants to take
her revenge from Clare.
Break friendship with her
and all other ties she shares.
Clare is in no mood
to set James free.
Or tell Susie about James
her only love to be.

A friend or love, Susie chose
her love to be the one.
Friends part and take their ways
while love is the union.
For Clare, her friends are her assets
and love is her real being.
She loves her life most with friends
like a queen or a king.

Are We?

Are we friends or just strangers?

In the wake of time
the colours of the rainbow
separated by a wish
or sixth sense.
Sail the feelings of our hearts.
Amusingly though;
who knows we're strangers?
Or friends at the fence.

Are we lovers or just good friends?

At the stop of time
our hearts raced to the end.
Swept our feelings
like a storm.
Into a whirling ecstasy
and vibes unknown to send.
Fusion of body and soul
way beyond the norm.

Yes! We are born to be lovers.

While I sip my thoughts
from the glass of my mind.
Questions may emerge
from our timeless past.
Could we trace?
Our emotion of the kind
which makes strangers
friends and lovers to last.

We shall sail though the tide of times.

Focusing On Sleaze

Opponent takes great pride in focusing on sleaze.
Good for his image waking up from a long freeze.
A chance to rise and show the nation his talent
like a key player of politics or a front line gallant.

His search revolves around a few loyal beaks.
At any cost he must get his hands on media freaks.
Then spread the news on the airwaves or wire.
That is more than enough to create a wild fire.

Upon the knife-edge or on the brink of disaster
the bench opposite seeks remedy easier and faster.
No stone left unturned and no doors unlocked
for the rivals to enter into an agreement or talk.

Nature of politics is that it creates sleazy air
for opponents to breed their kind of foul affair.
To wind up, old appeal dies, due to lack of time.
And a fresh sleaze becomes a scene of crime.

Cleo the Queen

Twilight, dawn or rise of shades.
Seen the games played dire or dear.
Know all the moves you've made.
To the ends of the Earth far or near.

Moved the king and the pawn
armed with envy and love.
Yet your show is plainly gone
to hide the scheme of trance.
Like a present large or mean.
I see in you Cleo the Queen.

Money and Politics

Cash for question is quite a useful phrase.
So is the politics as a money making trade.
Money is the mother of greed and power.
Politics acts the role, stands like a father.
Money makes the house of decision shady.
Where politics twists and turns like a lady.
Money feeds all known mouth of hunger.
And there politics lends a hand stronger.

So, what if money stops to flood the plain
of drought stricken politics is sure to drain?
Longer the shortfall of funds to the parties.
No more sweet talks from political smarties.
Still it is the money that makes the world go.
And politics is there to hype it high or low.
Money makes a manor or a hut, heaven or hell.
But it can't buy honesty and politics can't sell.

A Sweetheart

A face to win my heart, is so hard
to find, from countless faces that I see
in my dreams, day and night.
From the dark corner of my desire
a beacon of search shall rise to focus
upon my notion of quest for a sweetheart.

Could that unique gesture of hers be lost
in the mishmash of the web of wills?
And her enticing face just hidden
in the depths of my desire.
Where my heart sinks deep inside
in the pool of her platonic love.

At ease and peaceful I may look
but there is a storm of scarce faces inside.
This hunger, for one look of hers
one day will steal all my zeal of life.
So restless I am dying to seek
a lifelong hold of forsaken love.

Age of ‘ To You... From Me’ has gone past.
Time is now to say this once and for all
that she is the one I long to be with
and I will give up all I have and every one.
So now she must come face to face
and be my valentine this year and forever.

Bonding of Hearts

Heart is the king in the realm of emotion.
And like a friendly nation it relates with
the other hearts beating in tune with care.
Tries to bring close for bonding of hearts.

At times mind takes control of most acts.
And feelings drown in the depth of tears.
Whereas hearts rely on their beats to gain
vigour and courage to bind souls in fears.

Out of ties stands an army of lonely souls.
Set to attack any time during missed beats.
Attraction or love ceases to bind any more.
And hearts fail to link feelings in its feats.

Trying to fill the growing needs of love
as the time gets to a point of no return.
The roots of eternal link grow deeper
for lovely ties called bonding of hearts.

A State Called Singularity

It is in our conscious
that we live and bear in mind
gain or loss of our thoughts.
When death claims
the soul of a being.
Core of this world
slips away in the black hole.
Light of our sight dissolves
and hearts forget to beat.
That's when death swallows life.
Where time stretches and melts
into a state called singularity.

Body decays and soul lives.
But belief says mind rules
in life after death.
Being conscious is to live
and what of death after life.
Is it to be unconscious
memory has to banish?
When and where life meets death
to fuse with unconscious mind.
And if so;
what is this form?
Is this the form of dark matter?
Where souls live
in the state of nothingness.

When memory is focussed
into a point of charge.
And thoughts are sucked
into dense black hole.
That's when consciousness awakes
and there we see
in primordial dark.
Plasma of matters known
and unknown from the spark
of chaos and destruction.
A flow of double-edged
spark of molten time.

From the time of creation
whence the life of matter began.
We can only be sure
of the state of oblivion.
It is in essence the ability
to perceive and feel.
The tenderness of living being.
This is what we can predict
in time and space.
What we can simply call?
A place of oblivion
or a state of singularity.

Peoples of the World

Peoples of the world
exist at the edge of peace.
Cry at the options heard
and stand as an army at ease.

Why not listen to their plight?
Their cry for help you can hear.
With kind heart and devil's fright
love soaks the shadow of fear.

Peoples clinched to their lives.
Hands of death now seek revenge.
Tired husbands and cool wives
promise their dreams to change.

Look at the gardens of hope
here grows the apple of peace.
Also live here slaves of greed.
It's time for the tide to retreat.

A Friend

What is a friend...?
Refusing to lend a hand
in times of need.
Facing the hate of hurt
knows not how to get
a friend to heed.

Recalls the time
of dire distress.
And wailing of a friend
when in pain.
Facing him on test
his patience did not bend.

A friend or a fearsome foe?
Just one way to go.
From the other
to choose one.
It is not an easy
path to tread or run.

Bonding of a mind
or support of a soul.
All for one
and one for all.
It is well known
a true friend is never a foe.

You can See

Now you can see what I have become.

By your love, torn to shreds
woven like an emotional web of a man
glued to the tune, of the song
that you sang.

My heart broken, like a piece of glass
and dispersed, like grains of sand.
Silence struck cries and tears
but made no bang.

You don't remember but I can.

Pages of Time

Let the books of past speak
and pages of time to turn.
Secret of ocean shallow or deep
and land of future to learn.
Mystery of ages love and romance
war of wisdom in peace and trance.
Sailing of ships sinking or adrift
voyages of unknown glued to the rift.

Between the peaks of the tidal wave
or hidden treasure of Solomon's cave.
Buried corpse of the past rises to heaven
holding the hands of unknown maiden.
Heavenly bodies are destined to speak
and archives of science are about to learn.
Who they are and what they try to seek?
But they have forgotten themselves in turn.

A Feasible Discord

She loves to create
sound point of view
just to win over her case.
Such as
it is best to sleep
on your back
than to sleep
on left or right of your face.

She bites her nails
while she talks
eating half of the words.
She loads her knees
beneath her hands.
While my forehead
floods with
the ridges of crease.

Tricky scenario
comes into being
where possibility goes out
and surety comes in.
Dispute takes a shape of
much needed treaty
and discords
changes to harmony.

A feasible discord
may become a rule of life
and compromise
a norm.
She may stop
focussing on her habits
and I may tear off
the pages of moaning form.

Eyes of Love

Looking through the eyes of love
so pretty, a woman I see.
Waiting just for me
to share my destiny.

She may be like a shadow
that I may not see.
And when she is with me
she either loves or hates to be.

She isn't the mirror of my dream
and I am not about to scream.
She could still be the soul of my life
and I swear to make her my wife.

She'll be the focus of my love
and I'll be true to her till I die.
As I see through the eyes,
in the eyes of love, she'd lie.

I Think...

I think life is like faces of the Moon.
It changes as the time slips away.
I think love is like candy floss.
There is no hurt if handled with care.
I think happiness is like the sunshine.
It's marred by the clouds of sorrow.
I think faith is like a budding vine.
It grips all fears wide and narrow.

What if life betrays and tries to end?
Or just loses the will to carry on.
And without love; how could the heart beat?
Stop love and there is no passion or heat.
When tears drip through the edges of a smile.
And a sunny day suddenly turns black.
When there is no one to turn to.
Not even fears and worries to meet.

Is death really the end of it all?
Then what about the life after death?
Doesn't love of life need a living soul?
So use the deeds of delusion and myth.
There is always a warm welcome
just waiting on the other side of rebuff.
Disregard the keenly felt concern
and lose all your zeal for yourself.

But life is where belief tends to be
and bears the fruits of wise living.
Lust for life is really longing to love.
And thoughts are what I try to link.
But within the hidden chain of wishes
my hope revives and desires grow.
My beliefs, reasons, feelings and senses
shapes the words of what I think.

Free as a Kite

Free as a kite on the string in the air
pulling the cord of love in my share.
Can't see what is that makes her run.
I look for love, not prowling for fun.

So keen to invite her for a cosy meal.
Attend to her needs with utmost zeal.
She flies a kiss and sometimes none
leaving me alone all deeds undone.

I share her humour and cynical views
make an effort to find other avenues.
But she does not give in and concede.
In that state there is no way to succeed.

I keep trying and hope that some day
she will come to my embrace and say.
'I love to marry you for what you are.'
I'll be the luckiest man on Earth thus far.

The Future

If you do not care to live for the future.
Then the future will not live for you.

You can also see where the future lies?
Buried here in the graveyard of today.

But the past has died and it's now reborn.
To find oath for the present to be sworn.

Now is the key to the past and the future.
So proclaim that future is here and now.

Let There Be No Secret

Let there be no secret
between us.
Not even a thought
that permits
to infuse
doubts of the kind
to reduce
depth of feelings in love.

I sense there is a touch
of grief on the scene.
Longing to lie
in between.
But she is quiet
not willing to share.
I am worried
to tell I do care.

I am like an open book
and she declines to read.
My hunger speaks
but she fails to feed.
No tears flow
to flood her heart.
And when it comes
I have to live apart

She is too good
to forget.
I never hide my love
even when upset.
She stays cool
that is a fright.
Her secret hurts me
all through day and night.

Rampant Life

Rampant life is like a thirst.
Its peak, raised by on set of times
to bear the strain, of outburst.
Search in sequence causes of crimes.
Its trough, filled with steam of passion
tied to a spool of naked wire.
Start life as a free mason
and soul spins around like a ball of fire.

At the edge of notion, trough and peak
cling to the conquest of life.
Incites flesh and bone to seek
wealth of love wrapped in kindness.
At the base of the Moslow's hierarchy of needs
the core of social peace is to rest.
Time for the Pavlovian dogs for their feeds
a dish of frenzy and a bowl of fury to digest.

Justice On Trial

A case to identify an accused
to prove him guilty.
An eyewitness tells the court
he saw him at the time.
The accused running away
from the scene of the crime.
But DNA report and profile
points to an act of justice on trial.

How to reconcile
the problem facing the court?
Between the DNA profile
and the only witness.
The court is at liberty
to view the proofs with fairness.
On the one hand doubt of vision
and on the other weight of test.

If injustice plays in one hand
of the eyewitness
and proof of profile on the other.
Is there a possibility
that justice is blinded
by the proof and acts so vile?
On trial are the honesty and the force
looking into the eyes of facts.

A criminal on trial is really a test
to prove acts vile or good.
An ordeal of right or wrong
under the legal hood.
At times facts and figures
of the case distorts as fetish.
An innocent gets to gallows
blinded like the lady of justice.

Mystic Man!

Mystic man! You needn't fear for our soul.
Mystic man! Your magic is safe with us all.
We want you to know that you should stay.
Until we know you and the things you say.

Tried to sense the spirit of your words.
Mystifying they are but makes me sad.
Stigma of crypt sounds from your bell.
The greed of heaven and fright of hell.

We're trying hard to get to know you.
But it's no use you are still a mystery.
How could we know all your teachings?
And the sole truth you are searching for.

You are in a trance and we are awake.
If you keep quiet our hearts will ache.
In the wild some lone psychic will die.
Even before, we say to him, good-bye.

Prisoner of Time

Born free and put up to live by the rules of nature.
Caught by the clock of life like a prisoner of time.

Soul is the hostage kept inside the body as a guard.
Setting the ranks of resolve, from infancy, to climb.

Free from restrains and no legal frames to follow.
There couldn't be a land without the heat or rime.

The universe remains locked since the tick began.
Circling galaxies are on course till the end of time.

Honeybee!

When you gazed into my eyes.
You thought I was hypnotised
and in love with you.
What was the means of your resolve?
I knew it was not going to solve.
What it means to be like a honeybee?

Honeybee! Love means nothing to me.
It was just a way to make you smile.
Honeybee! Don't you remember me?
And how I think of you all the while.

A gasp of fresh air and you are here.
I can bear no more on this lonely shore.
And now I realise what it means to be.
Free like a honeybee, a honeybee.

I've lost my wings I can't fly anymore.
I shall return to you or die at your door.
Give you my soul and all my love.
Let me be your honey, your honeybee.

All About Manifesto

First and foremost politics is all about manifesto
and the promises that the politicians make.
An urge to show their skill of manipulation
and changing the directions in their wake.
Delusion is an act they play and gladly portray
to win next term in office without any break.

Personal greed lays a claim upon their pledge
to the people of the nation in wait.
And spin doctors try to soothe the wounded
hearts and minds but it's too late.
Devious acts have already awaken the revolt
and politicians get ready to fight for their fate.

The pages have hidden agenda beyond belief.
And moral correctness lay like a fallen leaf.
Creative resources are there to be used
for an account given to the public bemused.
Straight talks are far from their reach.
To face the reality they seem to be confused.

Who wins or loses is just a point of view?
For nation's people or a mere chosen few.
But the majority is really deaf and blind.
The power of speech that reaches the sky
are the screams, shouts and awful cry.
In the end winners or losers are hard to find.

Tease and Torments

Her tricks and jokes are not easy to share.
When she says to get it, it's hard to bear.
I draw to her arms and in her catchments.
When she plays hip to tease and torments.

No matter what I do, she gets her way.
I do not give in easily and try to be hard.
Then she plays tricks on me just to amaze.
At the end I throw at her my wild card.

I have tried to be serious, sober and grim.
Even shown to be completely out of trim.
Nothing works against her beguiling eyes.
She is a soul of affection clever and wise.

Taunts and tease never makes me at ease.
Distress creates a lot of pain in my heart.
For love I give to her like birds and bees.
Only way to live with her or else be apart.

The Difference Between...
He and She

Besides the obvious, the difference between
he and she, is like a throw of dice.
Resting on the facets of life kind or mean
she is a pool of piety once or twice.
Whereas he walks on a tight rope
but stands at ease ready to pay any price.
Like a spell she chants mysteries
whereas he splices his life, slice by slice.

She is intrigued by a play of chance
and he likes to win each and every game.
She is tormented by lively thoughts
and he? The bull's eye is always in his aim.
Enigma of ages moulded in flesh and bone
she likes to sleep walk in fortune and fame.
He is the one who takes a flight of fancy
whereas she dances like a flame.

He is only the one side of the coin of life
she is the other face to make it complete.
If she plays the means of creation
and he sails through the ocean of deceit.
Stress of journey on the high way of life
torments her soul day and night.
Where he stands alone proud and pleased
and she guides him through darkness and light.

She makes up for all there is in life.
He is so very much immune from strife.
One way or the other in life and death
he is there for her and she is for him.
Where tears merge with laughter
and life flows like the tick of time.
Obvious is the smile on the face of bliss
the difference sleeps at the edge of the wish.

Wedding Bells

I hear the sound of wedding bells even in my sleep.
It rings in my ears day and night, shallow and deep.
He promises to marry me, in earnest, some day soon.
Keeps me guessing for the day of our honeymoon.

Must I waste my life waiting for him to say yes?
Or break free from his hold without making a mess.
I know he would track me anywhere I care to go.
And turn nasty, treating me, just like any old foe.

His unjust silence is enough to break me into pieces.
So I must raise my voice against his empty promises.
Even if it brings tears to my eyes and pain in my heart.
The only way to be happy in my life is by being apart.

Yet after so many years together would I be happy
not seeing his face when he calls me to be snappy?
And his soft voice ringing in my ears day and night
for the things I do for him without the marital right.

Spoilt for Choice

Spoilt for choice
or struggling to impress.
The chosen device
seems to be in a mess.
From the top
the word is out.
Incompetent is he
so they shout.

Picked for the job
being the elite.
A man of money
standing on his feet.
When exposed
to be aided by a friend.
Nothing he can do
himself to defend.

A star of political pack
not to accept defeat.
Trial by media
and trodden under feet.
Is it a ploy to tarnish
his image and the party?
Promises not to quit
due to query of a kind hearty.

Agrees to be unaware
of the financial help.
But declares
all his interests himself.
On this point
he cannot resign
from the scene
and the rank he is in.

Breach Our Trust

Body breach hurts for a short time
and heals quickly like a past crime.
Whereas belief spreads its root, first
with souls, never to breach our trust.

Belief and trust vs. body and soul.
How to know the two joined as one?
Our faith is really the bullet of trust
and our body used as barrel of a gun.

Honour lives as an answer to breach
as a mark between right and wrong.
Distrust starts right from the belief
to teach and sing in tune of the song.

All in all, sign of a breach is in doubt
when there is a bias in personal gain.
Trust finds allies from inside and out
and a faith's key to the door of brain.

A Casual Kiss

Never knew that a casual kiss of this kind
could lead to and stir up such a deep feeling.

Each tiny twist and turn of needs I find.
Hurts love even deeper for the healing.

I wish to take back the kiss I left on you.
It is not easy to undo this kind of dealing.

Stillness fills my heart with utmost zeal.
My aim in life is to change this feeling.

A Guest of Distress

When I'm a guest of distress

and worries breathe at my neck.

When I'm in deep pain

crying for help again and again.

When the world seems the last place to be.

And even my conscience turns against me.

I see a light, a light of hope

shine like a morning star.

Shining through the sea of strife.

Just to soothe all the pains in my life.

Code of Conduct

For some code of conduct
is for others to obey.
The rules that run
charades of all lives
night and day.
They are all above norms
symbols and signs.
Not to copy their acts or mimes.

If their actions are checked
and their deeds
brought to notice.
Turning in their beds
spend sleepless nights
they seem to be fetish.
Their show of might
hits the weakest by night.

Freedom to live by rules
and manners to guide.
Is there any point
to be good and abide?
Is it better to be
a con artist of repute?
Than a devout genie
playing the flute.

So the code is made
to be broken.
And what of conduct?
Is there a limit
of its span?
Or the peak of its accord
reaches to the sky.
And code of conduct says goodbye.

Angel of Wisdom!

Angel of wisdom!
Descend from the sky
down to the hilltops.
To find they are sly.

Reach to the place
where, once you were.
Angel of wisdom!
Please take me there.

They haven't changed.
Would they ever?
You must show them
the way of just and fair.

You promised my soul
not to dwell upon fear.
Wisdom! They look for you
far and near.

They hate accords
and the songs they sang.
Didn't they hail
the innocence to hang?

Give them the light
the light of vision to guide.
Or leave them
in their coffins to hide.

Now that spell!!!
The spell of ignorance has broken.
And love light has touched
their souls forsaken.

Promise that you...
won't leave them in fear.
Now for their deeds
they all seek penance here.

Her Touch

With her touch she revives my soul.
And sends a shiver right through me.

There doesn't seem to be a girl like her.
Not in this world, one there wouldn't be.

How can a touch send shivers to infuse
in my heart that I can sense her and see?

I am the one who craves for her embrace.
She is the lock of bliss and I am the key.

A Firm Pursuit

I'll make you kneel before me
and if you do not bow.
You'll face the might of army
and a firm pursuit to the end.

I do not need to be so cruel.
Yet I've to be in command.
And you must obey the norms
of peace even in times of war.

If you dare to flaunt the rules.
The spell of truce won't ensue.
And all ties between us
shall cease to be without feud.

So end all your acts
and I'll forget the past.
Play the games in tune
with no trials to last.

Bride of Destiny

Is she a bride of destiny?
My bride!
She is the chosen one
chosen to be my pride.
My bride!
A girl of fate.
Did I meet her just by chance?
Or planned her to be my mate.

If future is the son of past
and past is to forget.
Then what does the future hold
for me and my bride
so chosen on the net?
She is a gift of past
to my present
and I have to make it last.

Should I look at the face
of fate or chance
for my bride to be?
Without her I cannot live
on my fate or luck purely.
And my choice of bride
left on some forgotten past.
While present is here to give.

My choice is the winner
but it's a matter of fate.
I met my bride
on a journey
from love to hate.
So who is to be crowned
the winner of bride
my choice or my pride?

True Vision

My eyes are a God's gift but not for me.
It's only made to see and admire him.
So I devote these to him and his love.
My one and the only true vision.

He thinks that I daydream but it is real.
And he even jokes and makes fun of me.
But I am stuck on one track in his love.
I could take his life or die for him.

Blinded in love and even in my dark days
he plays the game of love and hate.
While I play the game of losing to win
his heart by losing myself into oblivion.

Pleasure is mine even at a cost of patience
and to win or lose has no meaning for me.
As long as my vision is there for him
a sight of him would restore my dream.

Keeper of Love

How do I worship him?
Light a candle of kiss
on the altar of love.
Or kneel for his grace.
Why do I bear the parting pain?
Because I think of him.
And I want him next to my skin.
Oh my soul! My keeper of love.

He is not only dear to me.
I also love his distant look
and the way he runs my affair.
Talking about me far and near.
Doesn't help to raise my ego
and his tie is getting weak.
It may break if not soon
love plugs in the emotional leak.

Now and then I hear a knock
at the edge of my heart.
With each beat it reminds me
that my love is going apart.
Love to hate and hate and hate.
And what if that is the fate?
There only be my loveless body,
without my soul, having to last.

I am restless, with no call
from him, each moment of the day.
While he sleeps in peace
I die at each tick of the hours.
I deeply love this heartless man
and try to forget him and his attire.
No use, I can't get him out
he is my sole keeper of love.

A Good Day

In today's world of political correctness
one is wise to catch a golden sunrise
to disperse the staunch of the bad news.
Just above the heads that will roll
in the good old offices of power.
They are busy to shape and create
spark of events to burn
bad news on a good day.

Zero Hour

When it is time to leave at the end of the day.
When it is all said and there is no more to say.
Time ticks and heart beats beyond its power.
Then it is, when deed is done, the zero hour.

One is more anxious for the time spent in vain.
All works and cost count goes down the drain.
How to make up for the loss of special chance?
Fortune or good luck is not booked in advance.

Let the time extend for the exact action to take.
Right it is to favour and show, love true or fake.
Nothingness seems to be the basis of all things.
Whilst eternity guards the end of living beings.

A bit for zilch is not just a saying or a phrase.
Stands to put out events of nature or set it ablaze.
As it backs the birth of a villain or death of a hero.
All beings come into being from the hour zero.

The Difference Between... Truth and Reality

There is a basic difference
between the truth and the reality.
On the one hand truth is a complete
and absolute honesty.
Whereas the reality makes its mark
upon a piece of evidence.
Though both gets to the point
giving the same credence.

The problem arises when truth is made to fit a tale
or spoken with a piece of evidence to support the claim.
Then truth disguises to face success or prepares to fail
in the domain of degradation
or rises to the apex of fame.

In context the truth
faces an army of lies in the battlefield
where fictional tales are ready to fight
with their charms.
No matter what reality throws
at the dishonesty's shield?
Betrayal fortifies words
at the expense of veracity 's arms.

Heart of the matter is that truth
needs no defensive words
and needs no legendary wall to hide
from the fictional lies.
Such is the state of reality
that it holds firm with records
and proves its link with authenticity
of life and its demise.

Body Suit

Body is a gift
beyond our control.
In line with our customs
we change
wrap and form
in part or as a whole.
Body suit to go
with the entire range.

Rules to keep
and standards to meet
parties to attend
and dancing to beat.
All of these acted
to marvel the event
with the norms
of borrowed or lent.

Body by birth
and suit acquired
after birth with a cry
and live to laughter.
This is the goal of life
we must fulfil.
Body suit is on offer
for life before the kill.

Hello!

Hello! Said love.
And I found a reason to live.

I used to smile at love.
And my love was born out of a smile.
Have fun! I used to say.
Day and night, night and day.

My love is my whole vision.
Yet I fail to see my love smile.
Does she really love me?
As I love her all the while.

Hello! She smiled and said.
'I am forever yours.'

Get Ready to Face

Cover up your wrong doings and get ready to face
the wrath of the masses and outcome of their hate.

People's choice is not to oppose their will and want.
You must come clean in their favour or so confront.

Denial or pretence in public does not stand a chance.
Forces agree to punish the guilty to sing and dance.

Think of the moment when you stand face to face.
Your career in their hands trying not to interlace.

I Lost You

I search for the moment I lost you
and my passion for life taken away.
Your selfish love led me stray too.
Now, I long for your love each day.

I wish to please you as I've done before.
And assure you, I am a changed man.
Shouts in anger and screams no more.
Level my head with your heart if I can.

The time is to find a shared ground
to put a guard on our upset feelings.
Fly to roost at home safe and sound.
You are the one to start the healings.

My grief may seem to be out of place.
This is what I feel as a friend and fan
and hide my feelings to save my face.
I do promise to be good from now on.

Chaos and Order

For an order to take place
chaos comes into being.
Just like the view of creation
for cosmos the king.
And for control to take hold
disorder gets to be there.
Till the end of time
takes its turn, chaos and order.

Intrude in the works of nature
and witness the change in rules.
Chaos is ready to shape
strong mountains and weak granules.
Choices are there to make
anarchy to take or peace to break.
Use the tools to control
or pay for the troubles to enrol.

No options to argue or claim
the role of nature in this regard.
The conflict results in shame
and order lines up in the courtyard.
The nature is sad to see
how the order is obeyed.
Chaos after order
or the start of order after chaos.

At the two extremes of life
semantic of deeds,
good or bad, stand at ease.
Like chaos and order
life follows the rules
life after death and death after life.
It is also the rule of creation
cry at birth and hush after death.

The Other Day

Yes! The other day
it was so bright.
I saw a lonely cloud
from a land so far
hiding from the sunlight.

Yes! The other day
I could see a face
drowning in tears.
Trying hard to reach
the lost ones far and near.

Yes! The other day
I shouted. Just be patient.
Have no fear
from a corner of belief
to help, hope is here.

Not Just Love

Not just love; although other wishes brush
with my heart and soul to appreciate it all.
On the journey of my childhood and teens
even as I changed to suits from my jeans.
And having a kind heart I had to take care
of duties to look after other people's affair.
I liked the hobbies of other sorts to attend
as love stayed in the queue right at the end.

I produced a work of art in my infant class
no love, apart from a paintbrush and a glass.
Went to a primary school as a bright boy.
Along with times table many things to do.
Taught to spell and sing but no love or toy.
Learnt history, science and other subjects
but no lessons or talks about loving objects.
Just in secondary school I learnt about love.

Besides love there are other dreams in life.
Things like time, motion, space and stars.
Stare at the Milky Way and think of strife.
Fly at the speed of light and move to mars.
What else is there in life than surf the net?
Life is cute with HD vision or the superset.
Love is for the people having nothing to do.
For some love comes last as a rainbow hue.

Where do I place love in my string of needs?
Mainly I meet my need of hunger and thirst.
And then look to fill the need of shelter first
before the psychic and mental needs are met.
But love as a motivator sometimes succeeds
and conquers the need for hunger and thirst.
Fate of beings are to go forth and multiply.
Such is the rank of love in the line of needs.

When

When you came to me
brought me the sunshine.
I was lost
like an artist in his art.
When you came to me
all things were fine.
And most of all
a longing of love in my heart.

Oh! Why did you show me?
Those glamorous days
and romantic places.
Only to walk away.

Together we were the best
be apart and troubles invade.
Together we seem to out shine
the dark afflicted shade.

Union of Soul

More than even heaven, my only wish was to marry.
But with great regret our honeymoon has taken a toll.

Bonding of hearts and minds commenced in stages.
Next our thoughts and wishes began to merge it all.

Pursued by the arms of dignity, turned up a change.
Then in the name of ' I and me' laid a trend of call.

Life long vow to live together or go through divorce.
Body couldn't be one, could there be union of soul?

What's This All About?

What's this all about?
Her eyes glued to my face
she raised a point under the weight.
I held her tight in my arms
as if to squeeze it all out and replied.
Dearest it's in our genes
we are bound by nature to procreate
and leave behind our icons.

Why then I shed tears
and my heart becomes restless?
There is more to this bodily act
than just to grow and multiply.
She squirmed beneath and asked.
Is there no such thing as love and feelings?
Releasing her from my hold I pulled out.
Yes! Love in itself is a means to have children.

Resting her head on my arms she whispered.
So, why does the smile sparkle
and river of tears flow?
Pain of losses pierce through our hearts
and happiness shines through our eyes.
Turning towards her and with a lazy glance
I kissed her soft lips and said.
These are the signs of life by design.

So, what shall I call this bodily act of ours?
Loving to love or love to be immortal.
She sighed taking a deep breath
sliding up her silky slender form on me.
Absorbed in her body gleaming in dim light
I reposed and leisurely replied.
Yes! It’s love seeking to be forever
as our physical part of creation.

Invaders of Our Conscience

With the sword of wisdom and the shield of faith
they try to make us believe in their dreamy tales.
The implant of their views forms the source of light.
And they keep us glued to the words of fiery plight.

Scary plots, scheming villains and fierce dialogues.
All of these chained and baited for our satisfaction.
Tense suspense, high drama and thrilling conflicts.
These are their real weapons of mass seduction.

Just a look and we're hooked till the end of the book.
Our hearts and minds are willing slaves to their words.
These impregnated glitters of real life fictional truth
works as though they're bright beacons of knowledge.

So from the darkest and deepest corners of our hearts
either we love or loathe all invaders of our conscience.

Please Help Me!

In the middle of the night
I heard a pleading cry.
Her melancholy calls
still echo in my ear.
In pain she cried in vain
to release her poor soul
from the torment of this life.
A pleading cry; please help me to die.

She has lived her life.
Now birth awaits revenge.
Her death may not be
her long life's end.
While her life without death
has no aim at all.
The only reason she breathes
is to get real worth of her birth.

Wish to die!
Could it be real?
We all want to live.
Is it not the fate of life
to long for death?
It is a gift of science
and we do grow old.
Yet decay, as a result.

She isn't the only one
with a wish to die.
Others plead for death
because it promises
a life after that.
Prize for death is the heaven.
And a cry for help is the key
to the door of another life.

Love and Fury

My world of love and fury stood still.
There was no poise or peace in sight.
Then from the peaks of the snowy hill.
A stream of fierce and burning light.
Fell upon the dark side of accolade.
While youth and anger merge to glow.
And memories slowly emerge and fade.
In her heart, love showering like snow.

The torrent of love demands to survive.
Help the needy lips burning with desire.
Loving eyes look for the care to revive.
As her moves dance like a flame of fire.
I breathe for her embrace to stay alive.
Her sweet love for mine, her sweet love.

Like Fireflies

She is there in my memory like Fireflies.
Flashing in the dark corners of my heart.

No longer she is around, I still hear her call.
Trying hard to forget, has turned into an art.

I must look ahead and start afresh to do well.
Leaving behind lonely life and longing past.

Her memory is a slow demise of my soul.
Better it is, to find another and forget it all.

Reasons to Live

Wearing a smile on her lips
and tears in her eyes.
She showed me the way
to my happiness.
Which best choices to make?
And my reasons to live.

She may have been
a figment of imagination.
Or straight out of my dreams.
Loss of her company
makes me realise and feel.
I am in fact incomplete.

To live my life to the full.
I must look for the reasons
of why she had to go.
It is really hard to lead my life
without her smile
that made me happy so long ago.

How do I...?

How do I love you?
It is not quite easy to reply.
Yet, I will make you realise and say
about the things, you can't deny.
At dawn before parting with your dreams
I kiss open your eyes with a smile.
Your day echoes with my warm greetings
and lovingly I light up your dusk
with millions of hopes and wishes.
Whereas I adorn your longing nights with
lots of love, cuddles and kisses.
These are the things I do because love you.

Why do you doubt my depth of desire?
By now you must know I mean well.
At times I may be null by mouth
but my eyes follow you around.
Only for you I take a great deal of care.
Day or night I always love you dear.

At times I see the sign of sadness
in your eyes touching my soul.
And your tone of incensed voice
that conveys your feelings.
These make me wonder and think
if I have been doing the wrong things.

Love isn't just doing something to please.
It is also to show the ways and means.
Here I may lack the ways to show
whereas the means are there to be seen.
Still I will go on, doing and showing
right through my life, how much I love you.

The Weather

What could beat the weather in its extremes?
First when it is good and then when it is bad.
There is only one entity to beat the weather
that is a woman of politics turned a housemaid.

So the weather has its own ups and downs
and such is the case with a woman's nature.
The only problem is in the way they change.
Forecast one but there is no rule for the other.

Feel bodily hot or cold or face stillness or storm.
There is no escape from the outrage of nature.
But a woman can beat the spite of the weather
by being ten times cruel and callous to the soul.

The weather provides the ambience to carry on
and presents a sense of endless pleasure in life.
Whereas a woman of politics or a housemaid
continues to incite a feeling to make her a wife.

She...

She is the one who creates the reasons why
the world suffers but bears the pains to live.
She is the one to stir the cause of life to strike
even a wrong chord for the right sound to give.

She is unaware of the features she portrays
when seeking to fix beginnings and the ends.
Span of her nest of charm isn't far and wide
even then she isn't short of lovers or friends.

She is to blame for the loss of innocence
and the reasons of changing love into hate.
She turns off the rising flame of blissful life
and even turns a bright future into a sad fate.

Yet she is all around and in all walks of life
making sure that things are as they should be.
And she is the love and life of all living souls.
This world of God isn't complete without 'She'.

I Want to Know

I want to know if they live up to their names.
Or the Nile swiftly changes into river Thames.
I want to know if the sky is truly what I see.
Or my optic nerves are in fact deceiving me.
I want to know if all that I hear is really true.
Or has my whole grey matter turned blue.
I want to know if there is an order of human.
Or am I certainly a being part of no one.

Be a liar or rightly beat about the bush.
Can't change the flow of time by a push.
And the eye does not affect what is in sight.
It is the case that nerve can't see the light.
Papillae do not taste the sweetest of wines.
And our eyes can't see the ray that shines.
Such is the split in the creation of a man.
With an immortal soul lives a mortal can.

Why don't I rebuff all in the know?
And forget them all, friends and foe.
Belief is that they are born with a vision.
When they can't see beyond their beliefs.
Where is the crave for deafening screams?
Cry of people is not an issue, as it seems.
But threats from the back door are to heed.
I have to live with this knowledge indeed.

Hard it is to get fame with doom and gloom.
Then revolt is tricky and not so easy to carry.
Like a tall bride for a sweet and short groom.
It is hardly a match good enough to marry.
I could live with the knowledge that they
really are trying to cause a civil order to last.
But who is the benefactor of the lost souls?
I couldn't possibly say, you know the pitfalls.

The Windows to My Soul

A look into his eyes shows the windows to my soul.
Is he my true love, I think, but am I for him at all?

When I see him, I lose my being in his dreamy gaze.
Am I free from his hold or being set for next phase?

He closes the windows to my soul and makes me cry.
Tears don't flow on my cheeks but I surely wish to die.

Too loved he is, even dearer than my body and soul.
I am thrilled to have him wipe my tears and console.

Love is Blind 1

Love doesn't care cast and creed so they say.
And blind cannot see the peaks high or low.
Piety doesn't choose between night and day.
And mind isn't limited to think fast or slow.

'Love is blind,' it is just a figure of speech.
Or is it called because the way we fall in it?
Blindness is bleak yet we long to remain
held in love for as long as dream's delight.

Does it mean that hate is an act of vision?
Or self-spurn has picked the one we love.
Blind!!! When we can see that special one
and gladly give our hearts over and above.

Longing for love is written in our genes.
And this thirst is also a need to procreate.
A blind person doesn't lack the sense of feelings.
If it is love he or she sees his or her mate.

Quest for Peace

Land is the source of livelihood and growth.
Also it creates a rift between love and loathe.
A chaos and clash to give up land occupied.
Loss of lives needs a quest for peace to confide.

A need to survive, causes the chaos to evolve
for safe living, on the one hand a wall stand.
On the other side, poor folks plan to devolve
their present and future format for taken land.

Not possible, seems to be, a search for peace.
A simple way out is to remain busy at war.
A means to turn people into an army on lease.
Gains to be the flow of wealth from near and far.

Parties at war, suffer mental agony and pain.
Whereas others act kindly for their own gain.
Man, money and matter and pressure of will.
Through the house, pass this ordinance or bill.

The Difference Between... Silence and Quiet

Silence is an order of accord to restore stillness
and quiet commands a restrained and muted hush.
Curb and quash is another core feature of silence
that can't simply be sustained, ignored or discussed.
Whereas calm, gentle and serene follows the quiet
whenever a tricky line of attack on action is in need.
Silence is golden they say; so is the calm and peace.
Control is geared up for quiet so take note and heed.

When silence seeks refuge like residue at the base
and screams take control of tired and weary face.
When quiet is strangled like some rebellious force
with the help of a few unruly and disruptive souls.
When silent past, brings forth loud and noisy cheers
and quiet is no longer shackled or subdued by fears.
How could the silence bear pain caused by uproar?
When quiet faces mayhem from a far more and more.

What if blast warns to acquire control over harmony?
And clamour seeks to defeat the emotional serenity.
A shot in the wild may or may not break the calm.
But a deafening noise is enough to spread calamity.
Opposing quiet naturally stands a vicious line of rafts.
Prepared to strike sleepy hush in its guarded expanse.
Where there is a host of strident and thunderous echo.
There will always be a cry to restore silence and quiet.

So what is the difference between silence and quiet?
The answer lies in its meanings and contextual might.
And let silence be the defender of comfort and relief.
As quiet shows us the right way to slumber and sleep.
The primitive passion for the search of a silent night
must not be wasted beyond the protocols or discords.
It is wise and proper to enjoy the serenity of silence
without counting the cost of quiet, pride or guidance.

On This Day

Venus of my heart, I chose you on this day.
All that remains now is to admire and enjoy.
Lucky I must be, to find some one like you.
Eager to question my love but fails to reply.
Night of intrigue turns a dream come true.
Though neglect may blind the eyes of care.
In near miss or hard hit, in seizing my fate.
Never stand for my smile, turn into tears.
Even if I am at a loss, in the affairs of love.

Pleasure is a Search

Pleasure is a search for sensual happiness
to uplift the self-esteem of body and soul.
A need to nourish starved and tired love
for a change of stance, looking out for all.
Happiness is what all of us want and need
at all times, crack of dawn or at nightfall.

A change in mood turns into a lethal curse
and a broken promise runs a river of tears.
Dignity takes a dive for better or worse
while body shakes from unknown fears.
Moments of joy are shorter than sorrow.
Can't be certain if it would tick tomorrow.

Despair, grief and sorrow are never far away
and casual affairs always leave a loose end.
In spite of this try to reinforce inner-self
but there is no resolve or rules to amend.
Hunger, lust or just yearnings for pleasure
destroys a man, his mind, body and soul.

Life in itself is a pool of pleasure to live.
All that comes with it are the reasons why.
Persona, ego, charisma or personal touch
are only there to help and build cohesion.
Pleasure is to make use of each and every
facets of life without any choice or plea.

In His Dreams

I hear him call her name in his dreams.
Sally!!! Please do not go now he shouts.
Who is Sally? I sit up doubting it seems.
While my heart sinks and mind flouts.

For him to find love away from my hold.
Must be because of the way I care for him.
Says, I take him for granted like new or old.
Hardly meet all his love needs so it seems.

A lot of times he neglects my true feelings.
And on purpose he tries to see through me.
I hope he fails to act in all double-dealings.
Above all love of his dreams called Sally.

Fears I hide and act as a usual housewife.
Dusk to dawn and in each day-to-day life.
Why do I fear of being lonely and alive?
Since I stay in and he works nine to five.

Who Am I...?

Who am I?
Am I a body and a soul?
Or just body without a soul.
Who am I?
Am I a being belonging to someone?
Or others belong to me.

Who am I?
Am I a loving son
and then became a brother to one
or possibly two, three, four or five?
There are a few others living in my hive.

Who am I?
Am I a dearest husband to one
beautiful woman?
Or a father to those
I brought into this world.
At times all of these makes me freeze
at noon and midnight.
Makes me stand at the cross road
and shout like mad ready to bite.

When I have to be
one or more of me.
That is when I am not
what I'm supposed to be.
Most of the time I play the role
but problem arises when a son
acts like a father.
And a husband turns out to be
a nephew, a cousin or a son.
All these role-plays
becomes so meshed and woven
that I forget altogether
who I am
and lose my wits.

As a matter of fact
I should ask myself.
What am I?
Am I an organic being
or something inorganic?
If organic; a vegetarian
or possibly non-vegetarian.

Either way I would like to feast
on all the worldly relations.
After being a son
and growing through relations
at the end now called
a grand dad.
Then most of the roles
that I play in between.

Even so I take great pride
in getting to know myself.
And playing the roles
of many sorts.
Abiding by the various rules
of numerous relations
and carrying them with respects
in the church or in courts.
Who am I to raise an issue
of this kind or dare to quote?

Meaning of Life

A few weeks ago I'd sown a seed of Sunflower.
Hope it would grow tall just like the Eiffel Tower.
Well! It's grown and a giant flower's bloomed.
Within days flower is destined to be doomed.

Its yellow petals have fallen to the ground.
Scattered round the root they have found
love and affection where once the seed lay.
Meaning of life is simply death and decay.

The Power

The power appears in many shapes and sizes.
The first is the brain, a tool of diverse disguises.
Clout of wealth, sits at the apex of the crown.
Then beauty is the next in line for a showdown.
War of wills and lands of a nation is the strength.
Where control and command dances at length.
The influence is right to dispel the evil of pride.
And the words fight when the deeds are set aside.

When moral spark burns the pride of power.
When enraged dissent takes a form of fantasy.
There begins a battle between discontent and order.
To suppress emerging self proclaimed regency.
Poverty and pain then reaches beyond control.
And distressed souls in search of bodies at peace.
Power stands at odds with the weakest ready to fall.
Striving to regain their place in line someday soon.

Powerless and destitute, they may turn out to be.
Yet faith is their defence against all aggression.
Doubts may impede their progress and poise.
But they never fail to fight for their protection.
To submit under duress is not against their ethics.
Loath to live free within the limits of unfair rule.
So they grab a chance to go beyond their means.
Is it right or wrong to admire their efforts as seen?

Self-control is what our belief needs to acquire.
And there is a tick of time that holds the key
to the door of oppression either to open or lock.
In not too far distant the power shall concede
the right of peoples to hold fates in their hands.
Then a mere weakness may turn into a torrent.
Like a trickle of drips running a river to succeed.
And turn into an ocean of weak shearing the lands.

The Difference Between...
A Miser and A Mean

How does a miser and a mean differ in life?
Well! One is most grudgingly tight fisted
while the other is usually keen and poor.
In other words the miser is hopeless and sad
and mean on the other hand is an intended doer.
But both are by far selfish, crazy and mad.

A miser cannot see or hear the scorn and slur
even when rebuff of conscience makes him suffer.
And what about the anguish of a trivial mean man.
He is on the receiving end of sarcasm and disdain.
They are the talk of the social strata rich and poor.
Their hands are tied and their self-esteem is lower.

Still a meagre rich is more generous and kind
than the most giving miser, open hearted man.
Like the thoughts of a caring fellow but mean
gets to all than the views of the fairest miser can.
Whereas even a least but gentle and kind-hearted rich
insures the growth of civic deeds from its core.

Stigma and disgrace for a miser and a mean
holds true today as it always has been.
The issue is; are they part and parcel
of social and cultural scene serving our society?
And however differentiated, a miser and a mean
would remain the cause for lacking the propriety.

Under Duress

Under duress, an innocent man is accused
on the basis of his right arm being bruised.

He denied taking part in any such crime.
But he could not bear the bruise of the time

The weight of law seems to be on his wits.
No way out, beating is leading him to fits.

Above all, agree to a crime even if coerced
tolerance is also a crime of coercion shared.

Foolish Heart or Wise Mind

Heart is foolish; heart is crazy, emotional and warm.
Knows not how to score or resolve points good or bad.
Whereas mind is wise and doesn't sway with charm.
Not even in search of an affair or being happy or sad.

Heart is held to count for all that goes wrong in life.
And love stands to bear the seal of pleasure or pain.
Mind on the other hand takes credit or blames strife.
Knows only to shield or shed legacy of loss or gain.

Heart is the centre of emotional vortex, web and maze.
Lies here dormant creation of all human love and hate.
Mind may be in control simply under our earnest gaze.
Playing tunes to make us dance with the rhythm of fate.

Foolish heart or wise mind; we are all made to realize
thoughts, views, care and concern of feelings unknown.
Heart is there to stretch the truth with visual disguise
and mind makes up the loss of feelings overthrown.

Hedonism... Prognosis

My conduct portrays
the sign of how I feel inside.
Problems in life
I have always tried to hide
hard and agonising decisions
that I have to make.
To live a hedonistic way of life
and truly thrust aside
my pragmatic bond
with the world at large.
Restrict emotional surge
to rise and fall on impulse.
The sail of self control
shall uphold my pride
to the stage of self-actualisation
till it begins to gleam.
Class of needs turned upside down
with love at the bottom of my heart.
Life-long companionship of
'Till death do us part.'

Needing to be together
and the factors of hedonism-mix.
Efforts of living have taken
a toll and my life, at a fix.
Scared vows and jolted vision
is there to contend
with dogma of love
and affairs of heart are to end.
All acts of effusion have
failed to abridge
the flow of the river
of love is at a siege.

Hedonism... Diagnosis

Change entire point of view
of my way of living.
Heal all my emotional wounds
and feelings of my heart.
Grow a tree of decision
to bear fruits of love.
Feed the hunger of hedonism
like a wild dove.
Break free from the grip of wedlock
and cut all carnal cords.
Pick a clean sheet to write afresh
the advent of a new age.
A novel way to strengthen
my resolve, id and ego.
For the sake of pleasure to last
with all my friends or foe.

Meet all my emergent needs
for the pleasure of wants.
Humming the tune of love
plan for mating chants.
Factors of hedonism-mix
found and brought into play.
To end the misery
of living hell of day to day.
No mental torture to bear
and no duty of vows.
No boasting nymphs to face
and no wise cows.
Simply all I ask is
trouble free love in my share.
And a plan of hedonism
for me to grasp and adhere.

Hedonism... Aims

How to solve my problems
led me to these aims?
To lead a hedonistic life
brushing off all the blames.
First to get a clean break
from love bonds of the past.
To lose all gifts of wedding
and make divorce to last.
Second aim is to win joy
at all times to reach.
By spending years of my life
on the sandy beach.
Thirdly to get self-fulfilled
comfort in the long term.
As a result of my efforts
and a plan of pleasure to confirm.

Hedonism... Objectives

On course I proceed
to find ways and means.
To pull out all
the factors of split.
First factor in the group
is to make her leave.
On the closed terms
out of all the dangers.

To make my nest
as far as I could.
And start the wheels
of pleasure to go round.
No reasons and no regrets
and no tears to shed.
Under all circumstances
I must keep cool head.

Agree a plan of visits
if there isn't one.
Make no slip and try to show
that its all been fun.
Leave the kids behind
where they ought to be.
Their need for maternal love
is more that I can see.

Finally all tangible assets
I must take care.
Do my best to realise
my hard earned share.
These factors of split
will join to yield.
The aims of the plan of pleasure
in my life to come true.

Hedonism... Strategy

Made of two minds
at war with each other.
Has been the highlight
of my life for a year.
So I must try to balance
my inborn and learnt feelings.
By rational adjudication
of day-to-day dealings.

Tolerance stretched far beyond
the reach of a common man.
To soak my tragic tears
of pain, at all times if I can.
And by all means I must evolve
a scheme to lead.
By the use of an equal
blend of my Ego and Id.

I should search all corners
of my heart with delight.
And find in her
the seed of mental fright.
Look out for the features
that moulds a man into a slave.
Leaving behind the essence
of torture out in her cave.

With honest heart I greet
her moves to come close.
And send a few friends
to sniff out as a nose.
Good answer shall come out
to find a reason to change.
And set a guidance to match
all kinds of deals to arrange.

Hard it may be to find
a ground to help or hostile to her.
There is a need to judge
and face the challenge in hand.
Point out all the failings
to rule her zeal.
Till she submits her soul
with a long lasting kneel.

Grow slowly for sure
their affection and love.
To equal the force on their
failings and accords to heed.
For my wishes and desires
apart from being in need.
And gain pleasure and peace
the aim of hedonism.

Restricted Access

What lies beyond the closed Gate of Bes?
And a sign that reads ‘Restricted Access.

Is there a secret to hide from public’s eye?
No right to the owners to examine or spy.

Liberty poses more issues than the answers.
Free speech makes more slaves than masters.

Right or wrong must create a balance view?
Freedom for nations and not for a chosen few.

The Other Woman

When he talks about the other woman close to him
my heart descends to a degree of deepest concern.
As I recall, it was his charm and the way he looked
at me that got my heart thumping and I got hooked.
This is the worry that I have to carry day and night.
His charm pulls the other woman that gives me a fright.

I do not know why I always look for a tell tale sign
if he has lipstick mark or smell of perfume on him.
I even search his pockets for odd things like a note,
a letter or things very small or large, bright or dim.
I guess he must know that I am keenly possessive
but wishes to ignore all my efforts and entire whim.

To a man other women are prettier than their present
mate or captured prisoner of love, a woman like me.
A fact is that anything acquired with ease turns cheap
in a matter of days, weeks, months or even a lifetime.
So the only resolve is to have patience and act wisely
and make him sweat for each try, every cent and dime.

They say that jealousy ignites wanton wish of heart.
That is what I wish to make my man think and feel.
I ought to invite a work colleague to dinner for a start.
And try to hold his hands just before and after a meal.
This would make my man wonder what's going on.
With his raised concern I am sure to get a better deal.

X-Ray Eyes

When I stand before him fully dressed.
He darts in, his look, just to mesmerise.
Look, top to toe, he gives if I am blessed.
Probing for love through his x-ray eyes.

Burning in his extreme glare and gaze.
Forced to think if it is a passing phase.
How do I make up for his lack of care?
Like having nothing on under his stare.

I ought to block him out from my mind.
As if he does not exist I should remind.
And if he covers up his lack of fairness.
Call the oath showing to its blindness.

There is no hiding from our mind's eye.
Even when our fair sense says goodbye.
One way or the other his look I admire.
His stare at me works like petrol on fire.

Let There Be Peace

Amidst conflicts and chaos
let there be peace.
Amidst confusion and unrest
let there be peace.
Even at the expense of
deaths, murders and the rest.
They all claim.
Let there be peace.

Sacrifice and loss of self-respect
and no freedom to breathe.
There never is an end
to hand over and give.
If peace and freedom
are at stake.
Then mighty kills
the helpless and the weak.

Waging war to defend
is vile and sad.
To rule by stick and carrot
must be bad.
A show of peace is not
like hit and run away.
Or at best sit and control
people's affairs of the day.

Let us fight the war of wisdom
and come to our senses.
Create the accord of faith
that does not crawl over fences.
For the people, by the people
and of the people.
Not the pieces but the peace
let there be peace, only peace.

An Odd Scene

I wonder what is it that makes people talk.
Makes them to heckle or makes them to joke.
At times I wonder black, brown, blue or pink.
What makes them to sail or urge them to sink?
On the highway, in congress or in the church
goal is the same just an odd scene to search.

Just look at their ways and how they behave.
They promise all, past, present and the future.
Focus the lens of thoughts convex or concave
upon all acts of damage, hurt and adventure.

Then you see the dead, alive and to be born.
Crushed by their discretion in a silver bowl.
Discussed, judged, agreed and ready to serve
by the heads of power empowered by us all.

The Difference Between... Belief and Trust

The belief I have is the agreement
of my heart and soul.
Whereas my trust rests upon the silent
deeds of others to call.
But the difference between belief and trust
is that I stand alone with one.
Whereas with other I might falter and fall.

How to tell which one is rightly mine?
Trust? I might shun in contempt
and forget to get hold of my belief.
Could the trust be entrusted to those
who do not even try and attempt
to know the reasoning of disbelief?

Why the devils of disbelief surround
the soul of credence and consent?
Deceit in them I have not found.
But distrust shown by others
plays a part to brace my belief.
Till my trust in them becomes deep.

To pursue; what is mine to keep
given by nature or acquired by birth?
It's the whole being, a gift of belief
to enhance my life and a joy to live.
Then I search for the gem, entrusted
to them, who have trust in me.

Very Late

She was very late to share
the feelings of her heart.
Though, I had a notion
that she had a soft spot for me.

I did follow her to some extent
then came a sharp rebuff.
What else can I do?
Far from her, found a nest to roost.

She spoke to me the other day.
Have I been avoiding her?
And poured out her feelings.
No. I said, simply looking at her.

It seems that she played
the age-old game of hard to get.
I took her to be out of my reach.
As a result now we both regret.

A Matter of Taste

It's a matter of taste if a gentleman prefers
blonde over brunette or brunette over blonde.
In essence passion plays a part in his choice
of wish and want, his hate, love and fond.

Do's and don'ts are not too far from his reach.
At times his choice is bland even for him to catch.
He would stick from one to the other like a leech.
Until he gets kicked out as in a football match.

Try, he would but fair-headed are far too few
for him to get and fulfil his fancy and favour.
While brunettes are a bit too pompous in lieu
of other women so far not worth his endeavour.

Considered to be a gentleman in his prime.
Life long hunt for a partner in life and death.
So where does the preference lie in between
life and death besides the blonde and brunette.

The Difference Between...
Wine and Women

Wine is a ferment of natural blend of produce
and women... women by nature produces the ferments.
Wine? One finds oneself by parting with its company.
Women? One is totally at a loss without them.
Wine? Confines the senses to an extent of absurdity.
Women? Beguiles the senses with just a smile.
All in all, wine is intoxicatingly harmful for health.
While women seem to be quite risky for wealth.
One is totally at a loss in their company.

In set stages wine shows its true colour
when it gets to swamp the sleepy head.
Exciting it is to show the mannish effect
then it lays a siege of compulsion instead.
Graceful they are and have no limits of keep
but a lack of resolve is a mark of their nature.
Their warmth, placid and inviting feature
is their weakness rather than strength in kind.

A sobering thought never enters an intoxicated brain.
Wine not only alters the deed but also starts the pain.
Often sobriety and belief reaches a point of no return
when wine seeks an exit to leave through a safest lane.
What if women are eager to find peace and quiet
by challenging manly amorous and friendly fits?
They bear the physical and emotional burden for all
though at times they appear to be out of their wits.

Well! What more can we say about wine and women?
Rationally they differ but from a man's point of view
wine is effective in controlling male zealous demon.
Whereas women control not only hearts and minds
but a myriad of desires and wishes to mention a few.
In essence both are alike in keeping a man whizzing round
in an orbit of their chosen conducts, acts and deeds in life.
And if in doubt just drink your wine and ask your wife.

In Our Hands

In our hands are lines of fate.
Fame and fortune we make.
Take control of our lives.
Happy or sad, early or late.

When a line change
and good fortune turns bad.
It is fate to blame
deeds stay untouched.

But deeds go out of our bounds.
And no control over fate.
Are we happy or sad?
There is no way out of mounds.

Truth is written in our hands.
We are the keepers of fortune and fame.
But we write our fate with our deeds
and turn a wild luck into a tame.

Vision of Conscience

A lost soul in deep crisis
belonging to no one and nowhere.
Longs to hold inherited belief
in opposing house of ethics.
A quest for a true and peaceful life,
in reality, is a vision of conscience.

A broken dream turns into a nightmare
and true insight loses its glance.
How to connect and emerge
as a free soul in waiting to accept
the norms of pious life?
There isn't a better vision than conscience.

It is foresight that leads
us to dwell in war or peace.
But most of all it is our conscience
that focuses our efforts
upon the objects of losses and gains.
There must be a vision towards true belief.

Oozing Pheromone

It is the wonder of oozing pheromone that starts
a special love link between the opposite genders.
When received it is seized if pleasing to hearts
for conjugal vows to be performed by the senders.

Why then sometimes link breaks after a while?
It is due to the blend of the gender and its profile.
Somehow the scent or its air takes a down turn
in the rising heat of being together all the while.

Genders of the both sexes are keen to hide aroma
of pheromone by masking with man made scents.
This way they end emotional affect and drama
and no questions of promising love links or vents.

It is surprising that neither a man nor a woman
takes to heart or knows the miracle of free scent.
It's good that they are naive of the effects or else
they'd change the gene that makes the pheromone.

Slope of Times

Quiet beings on the wintry slope of times.
Frost bitten by the icy cold stormy chimes.
The Sun's venomous eyes pierce the head.
Root, family and brood, they all turn red.
Calm hits all, young, old, Adams and Eves.
Unrest blows through distress and grieves.
Fiery graves, molten mansions and sheds.
Lost lives of the forgotten oceanic heads.

Dead beings tread the conscience of time.
Boxed layers of cries sink in their minds.
Heart of meadows and soul of the hills
stain of the season and uproar of the mills.
They sleep with the pain of fractured bones.
Like doomed heroes blasted out of horns.

The staunch of rebellious dead beings
airs noses of oceanic heads in their cocoons.
Hidden silence reshapes and remoulds in fury.
Until clouds of conscience assigns a jury.
Table of discontent gathers all clever and fools.
Sowing the hills and meadows with seeds to growl.
Awakening powers drips into mouth of deaths.
The rivers of revolt feed the oceanic heads.

Dead beings on the wintry slop of times.
Aroused by the infliction of the corporate crimes.
Growing from drips, streams, rivers to an ocean
covering the plains and mountains of all entities.
Gather the divers claws of platoons to heed.
Rising revolt of beings plants freedom's seed.

Journey to Marriage

Madly in love and no end of journey to marriage.
Wish to go through rites in a horse driven carriage.

I can't bear to see him discard me like a gift-wrap.
Body as a gift of love and soul used as a roadmap.

My sanity must take control of his wanton desire.
Without wedding rites, no caravan of lust for hire.

Going through bad phase and out pouring of tears.
Couldn't solve this mess and remove all my fears.

You Have Something

You have something I want he said.
I eyed him saying don't be silly Ed.
Later, on my way back from school.
Thinking what he meant was so cool.

I am worried and somewhat confused.
He never gave me something to shield.
We swap our notes from time to time.
But nothing besides laughter or weep.

Could I be the keeper of his heart's feeling?
That shows joy of love or rage of hate.
I do not know what to do and how to say.
Perhaps I ought to leave it for another day.

My only possession is; body and soul.
No physical or material goods at all.
What do I offer to him in lieu of his love?
Love is what I shall give over and above.

Leaders!

Leaders of the day
now take oath to defend.
Fate of the poor and the rich
is safe in their hands.
They promise to their flocks
'you needn't fear.'
Pillars of state safely locked away
to howl and jeer.

In their hands war and peace
plays the game of deceit.
Guided missiles and atomic arms
to use in the name of defence.
From the house of people's power
words rise to a feverish height.
To fulfil the promise
or lose hope and still win the fight.

The laggards of the day
swear to be the lions
and demand a fair play
but fight for their dens.
Leave the swords and standby
for the art of charms to deploy.
Where are the men and women?
They fled the cities and the towns.

Like the soldiers, hills stand at ease.
While nations scream in pain.
Ripe is the rise of revolt
and people in rage come to a halt.
Spawn of culture and pride
couldn't grow before it has died.
Frontiers of trust set aside.
Death cries! Save the value of life.

Leaders of the day
now sworn to be shrewd.
All entities with stony face
glued to chairs indulge in feud.
Rumour of secret starts with a thud
and spreads on the face of the Earth
to infest the wounded heart.
To change the scene for the best.

Lament of feud and a cry of dissent
a push to unite, an urge to thrust.
The leaders and laggards meet for talks
to cast a net over doves and hawks.
Leaders of the day some famed and brave
some masters of mischief and others naive.
They play roulette with life and death.
Leaders rise from the laggard's ashes.

Never Met

Was it fate that brought us together?
Or just by chance we happened to get
from far to near and chitchat to friendship
then love to hate; wish we had never met.

For no obvious reasons we opposed each other.
In fact when I laughed you started to cry.
And when I needed your love so badly
you were out of sight and I was out of mind.

A classic case of mismatch of hearts and minds
from the first encounter to the last stumble.
I was sad and drowning in tears as you packed
your things and left me alone for better or worst.

Human!

Human! Human!
For the sake of humanity.
Come and save, save
human's humanity.

Listen to that child's cry!
Can you hear, hear?
Listen to that mother's sigh!
It's cold-blooded murder.

Human! Human!
For the sake of humanity.
Come and save, save
human's humanity.

Look at those millions?
Dead! They are all dead.
Brothers and sisters
father and sons.

Look at those gardens.
Where once roses grew.
Now grows hate and bitterness
and the number of dead bodies.

Human! Human!
For the sake of humanity.
Come and save, save
human's humanity.

Love is Blind 2

Love is blind; how could it be?
I see love in her eyes looking at me.
She incites me to be her sole mate.
She knows pledge is what I hate.

I read the sign of smile on her lips.
I see the slightest moves she makes.
Then how could I be blind to love?
All that she has, I see right by me.

Love is far too sharp and sleek.
Love is innocent, mild and meek.
Love is a vision of special kind.
Love is heart and not the mind.

Yes love is blind for others to see.
Lovers know what they like to be.
They long for each other's embrace.
Just yearning to be face to face.

A Wild Doll

A wild doll he calls looking at me.
He knows how touchy I could be.
Precious to him and all he can give
to me as a soul mate for eternity.

Just because I play to be wild in bed.
He does not see the tears that I shed.
I lose heart when he is cruel and cold.
A nightly stand makes me feel like old.

One day it would come to a showdown.
And I would not be a docile and meek.
A fierce row would take place in town.
It would not go away in a day or week.

This doll will remain wild as long it takes
to make him realize that life isn't a game.
If he returns my growing love and makes
me his bride, my pride and not the shame.

Lightning Source UK Ltd.
Milton Keynes UK
UKHW011503200119
335780UK00001B/2/P

9 781608 603312